The Incas

The Incas

Pamela Odijk

Silver Burdett Press

Acknowledgments

The author and publishers are grateful to the following for permission to reproduce copyright photographs and prints:

ANT/Grant Dixon pp. 12 right, 26 right, 33; Peter Shaw p. 15; South American Pictures pp. 9, 11, 12 left, 13, 14, 16, 17, 18, 19, 20, 21, 24, 26, 27, 28, 30, 31, 32, 35, 36, 37, 38, 40, 41 and the cover photograph.

While every care has been taken to trace and acknowledge copyright, the publishers tender their apologies for any accidental infringement where copyright has proven untraceable. They would be pleased to come to a suitable arrangement with the rightful owner in each case.

First published 1989 by
THE MACMILLAN COMPANY OF AUSTRALIA PTY LTD
107 Moray Street, South Melbourne 3205
6 Clarke Street, Crows Nest 2065

Associated companies and representatives
throughout the world.

Adapted and first published in the United States in 1990
by Silver Burdett Press, Englewood Cliffs, N.J.

Library of Congress Cataloging-in-Publication Data

Odjik, Pamela, 1942–
    The Incas / by Pamela Odjik.
        p.   cm.—(The Ancient world)
    Summary: Describes the world of the Incas, examining such
  aspects of their lives as herds and hunting, food, medicine,
  clothes, religion, legends, art and architecture, and wars.
    1.Incas—Juvenile literature. [1. Incas)   2. Indians of South
  America.] 1.Title. II. Series: Odijk, Pamela, 1942–   Ancient world.
F3429.035   1989
984'.01—dc20   89-39621
                                                  CIP
                                                  AC

10-9-8-7-6 5-4 LSB ISBN 0-382-098897
10-9-8-7-6-5-4-3   PB ISBN 0-382-242645

The Incas

Contents

The Incas: Timeline

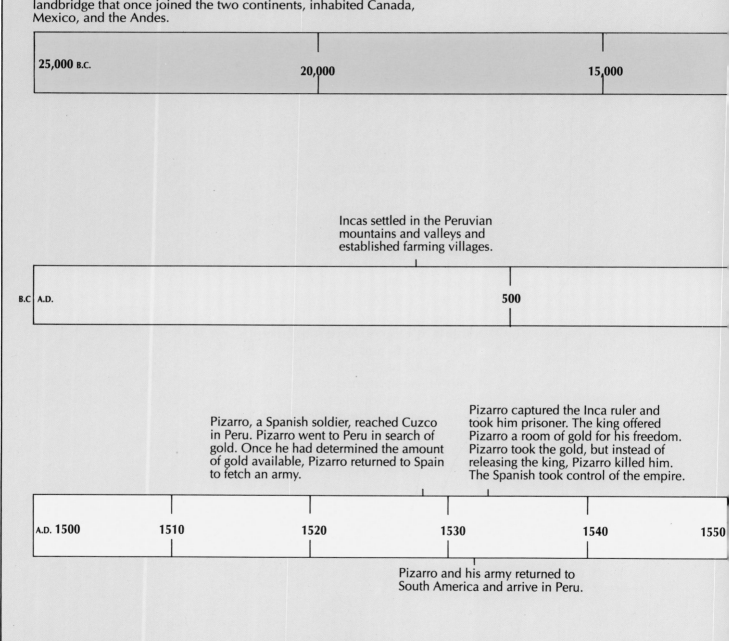

Hunting people, who had reached America from Asia by crossing a landbridge that once joined the two continents, inhabited Canada, Mexico, and the Andes.

25,000 B.C.	20,000	15,000

Incas settled in the Peruvian mountains and valleys and established farming villages.

B.C A.D.	500	

Pizarro, a Spanish soldier, reached Cuzco in Peru. Pizarro went to Peru in search of gold. Once he had determined the amount of gold available, Pizarro returned to Spain to fetch an army.

Pizarro captured the Inca ruler and took him prisoner. The king offered Pizarro a room of gold for his freedom. Pizarro took the gold, but instead of releasing the king, Pizarro killed him. The Spanish took control of the empire.

A.D. 1500	1510	1520	1530	1540	1550

Pizarro and his army returned to South America and arrive in Peru.

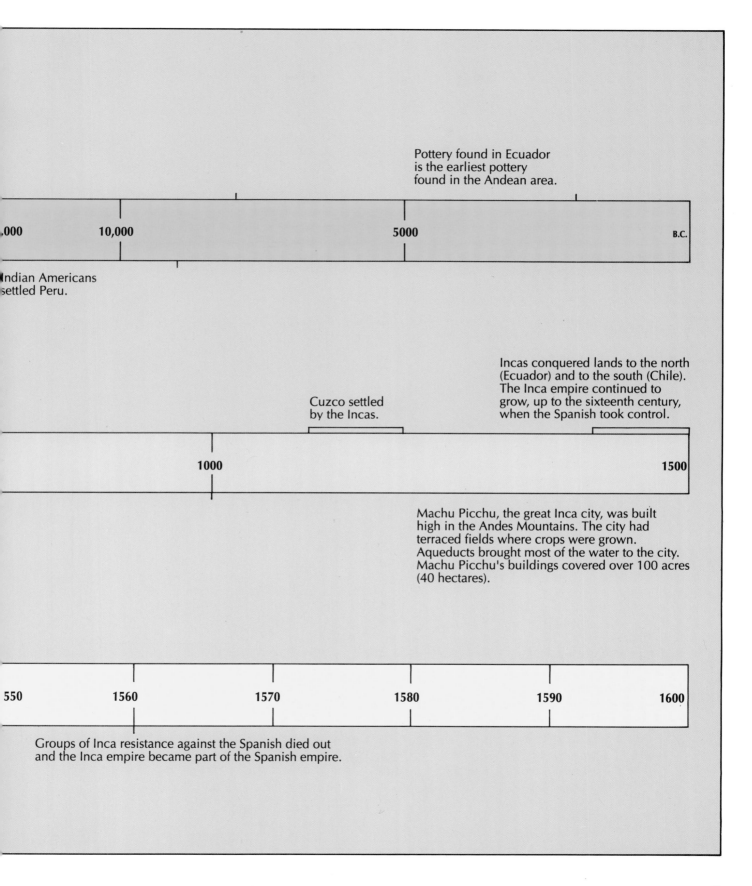

Pottery found in Ecuador is the earliest pottery found in the Andean area.

,000   10,000   5000   B.C.

Indian Americans settled Peru.

Incas conquered lands to the north (Ecuador) and to the south (Chile). The Inca empire continued to grow, up to the sixteenth century, when the Spanish took control.

Cuzco settled by the Incas.

1000   1500

Machu Picchu, the great Inca city, was built high in the Andes Mountains. The city had terraced fields where crops were grown. Aqueducts brought most of the water to the city. Machu Picchu's buildings covered over 100 acres (40 hectares).

550   1560   1570   1580   1590   1600

Groups of Inca resistance against the Spanish died out and the Inca empire became part of the Spanish empire.

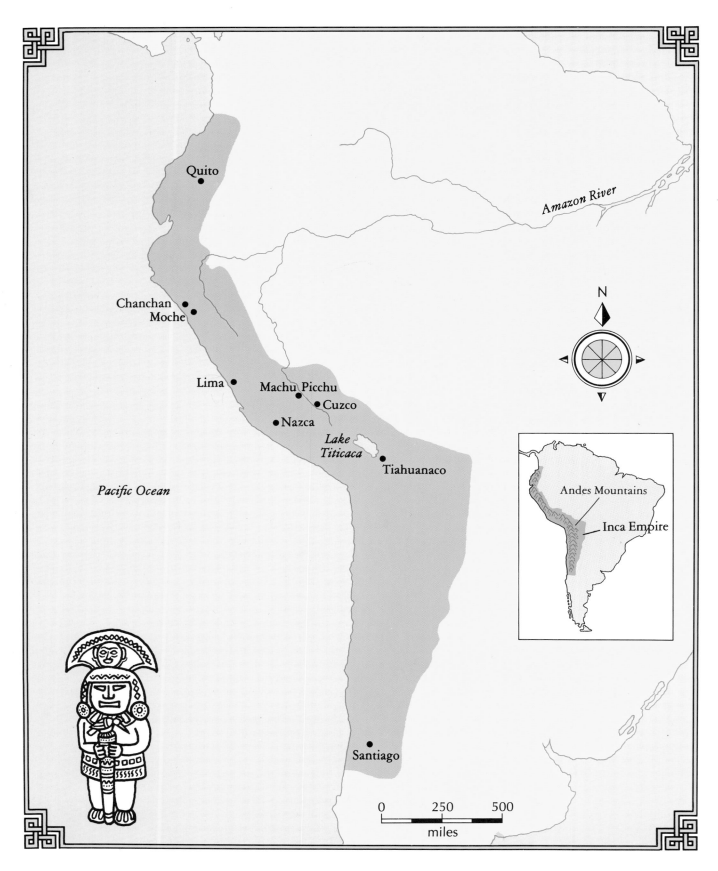

Quito

Chanchan
Moche

Lima

Machu Picchu
Cuzco

Nazca

Lake
Titicaca

Tiahuanaco

Pacific Ocean

Amazon River

N

Santiago

0   250   500
miles

Andes Mountains

Inca Empire

The Incas: Introduction

The Incas were South American Indians whose empire stretched along the Pacific coast of South America. It included southern Colombia, Ecuador, Peru, Bolivia, and parts of Chile and Argentina. This ancient civilization built great cities high in the Andes Mountains and farmed the fertile valleys that lie in between the mountain ranges and along the coasts.

The word "Inca" means chief or king. The ruler was called the Inca. Later, the term, Inca, was used to describe all the people in the lands that were conquered and ruled by this civilization.

The Incas' capital city was Cuzco, which dates back to the twelfth century A.D. The Incas began a series of conquests in the fifteenth century A.D., and within one hundred years, controlled some 32 million people of different cultures. The Incas allowed these people to keep their customs, religions, and traditions, but required them to worship the sun as a god, and to obey their new rulers.

Inca life at the time of the Spanish conquest.

The Incas were self-sufficient people and encouraged every group of people to provide for their own necessities in the coming year. What was left over was placed in storage for future need. Food, clothing, and shelter were very important, and the Incas tried to make sure that everyone had a home and that nobody went hungry. This basic aim of the Incas explains many aspects of their culture.

When the Incas conquered a new land, they assessed its resources. The land was divided into three parts so that part of the produce could be given to the Inca leaders, part to the sun god, and the remainder to the original community, including their own gods. Everything else in the community remained the same.

Most of our knowledge about the Inca civilization comes from the records of the Spanish who invaded the Inca empire in 1527. In 1533 they attacked the Inca capital, Cuzco. The Spanish were coming in search of Inca gold, which they had heard about from travelers. The bronze arrows, spears, and **slings** of the Incas were no match for the iron weapons, horses, and alien diseases of the Spanish and, as such, the Incas were easily defeated. The Incas continued to lead attacks against the Spanish invaders, but in the end, the Spanish and their allies tracked down the Inca leaders and killed them. The Spanish also tried to destroy the pagan religion of the Incas and to substitute Christianity in its place.

One Inca king had his Spanish secretary write the history of his father, Manco, as he dictated it, but this work, too, was later revised by a Spanish **friar**. We have also learned a great deal from excavations of Inca cities, particularly the city of Vilcabama at Machu Picchu, built in about A.D. 1000, which was discovered by the American archaeologist, Hiram Bingham. This city was not found by the Spanish and therefore not destroyed.

Inca Rulers

Inca Name	Spanish Spelling
Manqo Qhapaq	Manco Capac
Zinchi Roq'a	Sinchi Roca
Lloq'e Yupanki	Lloque Yupanqui
Mayta Qhapaq	Mayta Capac
Qhapaq Yupanki	Capac Yupanqui
'Inka Roq'e 'Inka	Inca Roca
Yawar Waqaq	Yahuar Huacac
Wiraqocha 'Inka	Viracocha Inca
'Inka 'Urqon	Inca Urcon
Pachakuti 'Inka Yupanki (1438–71)	Pachacuti Inca Yupanqui
Thupa 'Inka Yupanki (1471–93)	Topa Inca Yupanqui
Wayna Qhapaq (1493–32)	Huayna Capac
Washkar 'Inka (1525–32)	Huascar
'Ataw Wallpa 'Inka (1532–33)	Atahuallpa
Thupa Wallpa (1533)	Topa Huallpa
Manqo 'Inka Yupanki (1533–45)	Manco Inca Yupanqui
Pawllu Thupa 'Inka (c. 1535)	Paullu Topa Inca
Thupa 'Amaru (1545–72)	Topa Amaru

The Importance of Landforms and Climate

The land once inhabited by the Incas varies greatly, and includes hot deserts, tropical valleys, and snow-capped peaks and **glaciers**. The land rises sharply from the Pacific Ocean to a high plateau of 6,000 to 12,000 feet (1,830 to 3,660 meters), and then upwards to the Andes Mountains which rise to 20,000 feet (6,100 meters). In places this mountain range is 250 miles (400 kilometers) wide. A dry sandy desert strip is located along the coast where no rain falls. Lake Titicaca, a huge lake, is located high up in the mountains at 12,500 feet (3,810 meters) near the Inca capital of Cuzco.

Fertile valleys where food could be grown are often separated by stretches of desert or hills, and the steep slopes of the Andes only allow certain crops to grow at certain heights.

There is rapid evaporation of rainfall in the highlands as well as a long dry season. With physical labor, the Inca peasants built huge irrigation canals, which took the water many miles over farmlands to keep the land productive in the dry periods.

Although there were deposits of iron, the people did not know about its use. Deposits of gold were found in the streams and there were also deposits of silver and copper.

The dense rain forest formed the eastern border of the Incas' empire.

Natural Plants, Animals, and Birds

The diversity of the landscapes once inhabited by the Incas provide a range of plant, animal, and bird life. In some places hardwood and softwood forests with trees of mahogany, cedar, and walnut grow, and in the mountains, pockets of alpine grasses and other herbaceous plants are to be found. There are desert areas where tufted grasses and thorny bushes finally give way to barren sands. Animals include deer, **alpacas, llamas,** chinchilla, puma, monkeys, and rodents.

In the northern regions, vegetation ranges from wet lowlands to areas of tropical rain forest where jaguars, ocelots, foxes, weasels, otters, skunks, tapir, deer, and **peccary** are to be found.

There are many species of birds, with the condor being the largest. Along the coast are many seabirds whose droppings (**guano**) were used as fertilizer by the Incas.

Above: the peaks of Huandoy, part of the Andes Mountain range.

Jaguars live in Peru, where the Inca people once lived.

Opposite: llamas on the shore of Lake Titicaca, with the Andes in the background.

12

Crops, Herds, and Hunting

The Incas adopted the farming methods of the people they conquered. These people were well established long before the Incas came and included the cultures of the Nazcas, Mochicas, Tiahuanacans, Aymara Indians, and the Chimú.

The Incas were fine engineers. They learned how to control the water from the melting snow of the Andes, and directed it across the desert to farmlands using irrigation ditches.

They also diverted the water of rivers in the same way. **Aqueducts** of stone carried water across gorges, and tunnels were used through mountains.

The fertile valleys, including river valleys, were separated from each other by hills and stretches of desert. In the valleys, approximately forty different crops, vegetables, and medical herbs were grown. The most impor-

Incas cultivating potatoes.

Inca boy hunting birds using the bola, a hunting weapon made of stone balls attached to leather straps or string.

14

The steep lands of the Inca were cultivated using terraces.

tant crop in the Peru highlands was the potato, which was cultivated from its wild state to 700 varieties that suited different climates and purposes.

The steep Andes Mountains were cultivated using terraces. Corn and other crops needing a long growing season were planted in the lower areas; potatoes were grown in the areas a little higher up; and animals were grazed on the very high areas where the frosts made growth of crops impossible. There were communal pastures where everyone could graze flocks. Other crops included gourds, peppers, lima beans, sweet potatoes, cassava, quinoa (grain), various tubers, peanuts, tomatoes, avocados, cotton, and tobacco.

Order of Fields

The fields were cultivated by people using simple tools of wood, stone, and copper. Those lands belonging to the sun god were attended to first. Next the fields of the sick, the widowed, and the orphaned were tilled. Then the fields of soldiers or others in service and away from their lands were tilled, after which the peasants attended to their own fields. The lands of the Inca nobles were cultivated last, but were done with ceremony and chanting.

Animals

The llama and alpaca were domesticated animals from which the people of Peru obtained wool, meat, and other products. The llama was also used as a beast of burden. The finest wool was obtained from **vicuñas**. The guineau pig was raised as a food source.

Hunting

The ordinary peasants were not entitled to hunt game. This was reserved for the Inca rulers and the nobility who organized hunting parties during which thousands of animals were slaughtered. However, once a hunt had occurred, the area was not allowed to be hunted again for four years.

The **bola** was a hunting weapon made of stone balls attached to leather strips or string. It was thrown at an animal's legs so that it would wrap around them and make the animal fall. Then the animal could be easily killed with another weapon.

15

How Families Lived

The people under Inca rule usually belonged to the farming communities that had settled in different valleys. The **curacas,** or elders (who became administrators to the Incas), owned the land which was cultivated by the community. Families shared the land, grazing their flocks on communal pastures and cultivating the rest. Most communities grew enough food for themselves and only needed to trade occasionally with neighboring communities.

Houses

Peasant families lived in huts that had been built around a courtyard. Houses varied according to the region. In the central Andes, houses were rectangular and made of **adobe, turf sods,** or stone, and had thatched roofs. They did not have a lot of furniture. Hollows and crevices in the walls were used to store things. People wrapped themselves in thick blankets and slept on the floor. Outside the house, llamas were kept in a house yard. The peasants also kept guinea pigs for food.

The more luxurious houses of the Inca nobles were constructed of stone, with gold and silver ornaments decorating the walls. Many of their houses had small bathrooms with running water. Their houses were built in the best sheltered valleys and were surrounded by groves and gardens.

Men and women working in the fields sowing crops. This work was done in September of the agricultural year.

Men

Peasant men worked in the fields tending the crops and the animals on the land allotted to their family. Enough land to supply the needs of their family was made available each year. Young men had to spend some time in the army, and all adult men between twenty and fifty years of age could also be called upon to work on the Inca buildings and roads. Marriages were arranged for men when they turned twenty-four.

These huts of today's Peruvian peasants, made from adobe with thatched roofs, are similar to those once built by the Inca peasants in the central Andes.

Women

Women also worked in the fields, especially at harvest time. At home women made the clothing, prepared the food, and made rope, part of which was given as a tax payment. The family quota of llama wool was spun and woven by the women for their families.

All girls from eight to ten years of age were brought before a royal official. Some of these girls were sent to a convent, under the charge of an older woman, where they learned a variety of skills, such as the weaving of vicuña wool into fine material and the making of maize beer. At the age of thirteen or fourteen, the girls were again brought forward and some were selected for the Inca's harem or became slaves to nobles and officials. Others were sent to shrines as servants or priestesses, and some were used for human sacrifices. Marriages were arranged for the remaining women when they turned eighteen.

Education

Sons of the ruling Inca were educated at special palace schools. These boys were the future leaders, so they were taught government administration, religious rites, and the history of their royal ancestors.

Children of the peasants were educated by their parents and others in their community. Skills and traditions were passed on to the children.

17

Food and Medicine

Food

Maize was ground into flour for making bread and cakes that were cooked on hot stones. Meat from animals (especially those hunted by the Inca nobility) was dried and could then be eaten when needed. Guinea pigs and fish were also eaten. The everyday meals of the peasants were simple ones of stews made with vegetables such as potatoes, beans, squash, **okra,** and tomatoes, and spiced with peppers.

A maize beer called **chicha** was also brewed and drunk.

Feasts

The Incas also enjoyed feasting and dancing, and special ceremonial food was prepared for religious festivals. Great amounts of food and chicha were prepared by specially chosen women called "Virgins of the Sun," who worked in the convents. Gold or silver plates and goblets were used to serve food and drink on these occasions. Food was placed before the nobility on little mats.

Medicine

Priests were the official medical people who prescribed bloodletting, fasts, dieting, and bathing for certain illnesses. Herbs and plants, such as tobacco, were used for medicine. Coca leaves were also gathered and dried, mixed with lime and chewed. Cocaine was extracted from the leaves of the coca plant and used to ease pain. It was used in surgical operations performed on people injured in battle. These operations appear to have been carried out quite successfully. A drink was also produced from the stem and bark of a vine. It was called *yajé* and was thought to have healing powers.

However, the native medicines were useless against the diseases brought into the area by the Spanish. These were European diseases that the people of the South American continent had never been exposed to before. Hundreds of people died from smallpox, measles, malaria, and influenza.

Maize was one of the main Inca crops. Here the maize crop is being harvested in May of the agricultural year.

Clothes

The clothes worn by the ruling Incas and the peasants were all made from cotton and wool. Peasants clothing was very simple, but clothing of the rulers and nobles was made of the finest cotton and wool. Valuable material called **kumbi** was woven from fine vicuña wool and made into garments worn by the Inca and his family and priests. Cothing of the nobles and rulers was also brightly colored and decorated with feathers, embroidery, and metal sequins.

A symbol of rank was the **llautu**, a narrow band of many colors wound around the head and held in place with a scarlet woolen fringe (called a maskapaicha). Strands of the fringe were enclosed in little tubes of gold. Above the llautu, three rare birds' feathers were worn. Gold disks were worn in the ear lobes and on the chest.

Material for clothes was woven in simple portable looms and woven so that the pattern was identical from both sides. Hair of animals was also woven with the wool to make the fabric stronger. Bright patterns were woven into fabrics. The dyes were made from plants and minerals.

Wool from llamas, shorn every year, was given to families according to need. From this wool women could spin and weave cloth. This woolen cloth was necessary because the mountain air was very cold.

Cotton was supplied to people according to need also in the warmer low country areas. The clothes of the common people were very simple. Men wore wide bands of cloth around their waists and hips. They also wore a jacket which was a bit like a **poncho**. It was a large piece of cloth with an opening in the center for the head. Women wore long dresses and tied sashes around their waists. In the cold weather, both men and women wore shawls or cloaks, which were fastened with pins or brooches.

Women sometimes wore a veiled headdress

Inca poncho, from Cuzco, Peru.

which hung down their backs. Hair and head-dress styles differed in each part of the country.

Everyone wore sandals and shoes of leather or plaited grass.

Religion and Rituals of the Incas

Legend of the Beginning of the Inca

Primitive Indian people believed that their ancestors emerged from holes in the ground. These holes were called **paqarina,** or places of origin, and were regarded as shrines. Religious ceremonies were held at these places. Descendants went to these places to restore contact with their beginnings.

The Inca paqarina was at Paqari-tampu near Cuzco. Here there were three caves. According to the legend, the founder of the Incas, Manco Capac, emerged from the middle cave with his three brothers and four sisters. Ten groups of people emerged from the other caves to join them in a journey lasting many years. Finally they settled near Cuzco and prospered.

Inca gold mask depicting the sun. The Incas believed that their emperor was descended from the sun god.

Some Inca Gods and Goddesses

Name	About the God or Goddess
Inti	The sun god, from whom the Incas believed the king was descended. This was the main god who was served by many priests and "chosen women." This god owned most of the land and flocks and received the richest gifts. White llamas were sacrificed to the sun god.
Mamaquilla	Moon goddess and wife of the sun god.
Pacha-mama	The earth mother.
Sara-mama	The maize mother.
Illapa	The god of thunder, master of hail and rain. Llamas with various colored coats were sacrificed to him.
Viracocha	The creator god.

Peasant Religion

The Pacha-mama, or earth mother, was worshiped. The Incas thought that she protected them and their flocks. Idols and shrines or any items used in worship were called **huacas.** A huaca could also be a mountain, a rare animal, a deformed person, a rock, or the spirit of one of these things. Each family possessed **amulets,** called **conopas** or chancas, which varied from one area to another. These items were also huacas. They ranged from unusual stones to beautiful **talismans.** Among these were llama-

Opposite: Inti Raimi Pageant – Festival of the Sun God.

shaped figures with a hole in the back. It is thought that offerings were put in the hole and placed in the fields in the hope that the earth mother would increase the flocks. Others were shaped like maize and offered to Sara-mama, or maize mother. Other conopas were buried in secret places in the hope that the gods would protect the community.

Some piles of stones were also huacas. The Indians added more stones to these piles and often left other small offerings there. (The Spanish later planted crosses on these piles.) Huacas often became sacred by being connected to the Inca rulers. A house might become a huaca because an Inca noble lived in it; or a place might become sacred because an Inca noble had a dream there and ordered the spot to be made sacred.

Priests

There was a well-organized hierarchy of priests. Older men who could no longer work in the fields but whose knowledge was valued often served the local temples and huacas. There were also magicians and witch doctors and healers.

The New Religion

The great gods of the Incas were the powers of nature, especially the Sun, Inti, and the Moon, Quilla. Other important deities were the Thunder and Rainbow gods and the bright planets.

Over them all reigned Viracocha, the Creator. He was both father and mother of the Sun and Moon. He was often thought of as an old man with white hair and beard.

Pachacuti appointed priests, had temples built, and had prayers written for Viracocha. The Inca armies then went out convinced that they had a divine mission to conquer lands in the name of Viracocha.

Conquered people did not have to give up their own gods, but they had to worship the Inca gods and provide these gods with food, land, and labor.

Burial Customs

Bodies of the Inca rulers were embalmed and placed in the Temple of the Sun. They were dressed in fine clothes and were seated on chairs of gold, with their arms crossed and their heads bowed. Gold ornaments adorned them. At certain festivals these bodies of the ancestors were brought out into the square for further ceremony. When an Inca died, his palaces were abandoned (except one which was opened and guarded because of the belief that in time the Inca would return).

Community ancestors were also worshiped, and the bones and bodies of these people (called malquis) were preserved in ancient burial places (called machays). Sometimes these bodies were covered in tunics and plumes.

Peasants buried their dead in caverns and tombs. When the Spanish insisted upon burying the dead underground in cemeteries, the peasants were horrified. They imagined that their ancestors would be exhausted and crushed by the weight of the earth.

Sacrifices

Llamas were the animals most frequently sacrificed, although men, women, and children were sacrificed whenever it was thought this was needed. Most of the children who were sacrificed were buried alive, although some were killed in other ways. Animals were slaughtered on a sacrificial altar. Food, woolen garments, special wood, and baskets of special leaves were sacrificed by being thrown into a fire.

Religious Festivals

Raymi   This festival was for the glory of the sun and was very important to the Incas. Many ceremonies, lasting from a few days to several weeks, took place, and they were related to solstice, harvest, reaping, and the paying of taxes.

The Inca and his relatives (in procession according to rank and age) would go to the appointed place and wait barefoot for the rising sun. When it appeared they would kneel down, stretch out their arms, and acknowledge it as their father and their god. The Inca would then fill two goblets with wine, one for himself and one for the sun. The contents of the right-hand goblet would be ceremoniously poured on the ground for the sun to drink.

A sacred flame was lit using a mirrored surface and dry cotton, and it was entrusted to the care of the Virgins of the Sun.

Sitowa This was a great festival held to chase away evil spirits which might threaten a town. Everyone, including the army, would assemble and chant words such as "Sickness, disaster, unhappiness, leave us." While the chanting increased, armed warriors would run along the four roads leading out of the city, chasing the evil spirits to a fixed distance from the town. Here spears would be stuck into the ground as a barrier. The warriors would then bathe in the rivers to "wash away the evil."

People would come out of their houses shaking out clothes to represent the shaking out of evil. At night there was feasting and dancing with everyone washing away the evil in the river.

Men with lighted torches would chase the spirits of the night in the same way as the warriors had done.

Every household would prepare a paste from maize called sanko. This was rubbed on their bodies and on the steps of their houses to ward off illness and weakness. The statues of the Inca gods and the household gods were brought into the streets and rubbed with sanko. So was any huaca.

White llamas were then sacrificed and the sanko mixed with the blood of the sacrificed beast. Every man, woman, and child ate some of this as a sign of communion with their god.

Christianity

In later years, the Spanish forced Christianity on the native people. The people were required to attend Christian masses and were whipped for any singing or dancing, or for following any of their own customs. People were also sent away or had their heads shaved if they would not become Christians.

Tomb of Inca ruler Pachacuti. Rulers were embalmed and placed in the Temple of the Sun.

The Inca king and his nobles – the king ruled the vast Inca empire with the help of these officials.

The Incas had no system of writing and therefore no written laws. They kept law and order by controlling everything and everyone very strictly.

Inca Society

There were three classes in Inca society: the nobles—including both those who were "Incas by blood" and those who were "Incas by privilege," and peasants.

Inca Society	
Incas by Blood	Those who were blood relatives of the Inca. Since the Inca had several wives, he also had many relatives. The people in this class could become priests or lead the armies. They were also given the best land.
Incas by Privilege	These were people who had been rulers or chiefs in the lands that the Incas had conquered. They had less power and were not given as much as the Incas by blood. However, they helped the Incas rule the conquered lands.
Peasants	The common people. This group included farmers, fishermen, and conquered people.

Inca Administration

The Inca

The Inca was always a man. He was thought to be a child of the sun god. Everything and everyone belonged to him and he was worshiped as a god.

Suyuyuq Apu (Lord of the Suyu)

The Lord of one of the four regions of the Inca empire.

Hunu Kamayoq

Governor of a province with 10,000 families.

Waranq Kamayoq

Head of 1000 families.

Pichqa Pachaq Kamayoq

Head of 500 families.

Pachaq Kamayoq or Curaca

Head of 100 families.

Pichqa Chunka Kamayoq

Head of 50 families.

Chunka Kamayoq

Head of 10 families.

Pichqa Kamayoq

Head of 5 families.

Pureq

Head of 1 family.

Special Secret Police (called tokoyrikoq)

These people were like spies. They had to make sure no rebellions began and that taxes were being paid properly.

Mitmaq or Mitamaes

These were groups of people loyal to the Inca rulers who were transplanted into a newly conquered area.

They helped indoctrinate the local people and warned Inca rulers of rebellions.

Yanacuna

Slaves.

The Army

Inca officers led and administered the army. People from groups conquered by the Incas made up the army. All males had to serve in the army. Huge warehouses were set up at regular intervals to shelter and supply troops as they moved about the country.

Garrisons were situated throughout the empire to stop rebellions, and the soldiers at these garrisons were from areas that differed from the one in which they served.

If a rebellion occurred the army would attack. The rebel leaders were taken back to Cuzco and humiliated. Sometimes they were tortured and killed. Those killed had cups made from their skulls and drums made from their skins. The people of the area were then forced to give up land and herds.

Taxes

These were of two kinds:

Types of Taxes

Mit'a This consisted of a number of days labor to be served in the army, in personal service to the Inca, or on public works.

Farm Tax Members of the ethnic groups were required to work on the farms or care for the llama and alpaca herds on their own lands on behalf of the Inca. Some of the produce went to the government and the rest was kept by the people who did the work. However, no group was allowed to have more than it needed for the next year. The state stored what was left over to be used in times of famine or drought.

When a member of the Inca nobility visited a province, he decided how the province would be managed, such as what public works would be done and what kinds of punishments were needed.

Justice and punishment were carried out according to the traditions and customs of a province. This varied from place to place. Governors sat as judges, but very little is known about how a punishment was decided, except that torture and **divination** were used.

Theft was regarded as a serious crime and thieves were beaten with a stone. If they were found guilty a second time, they were beaten to death. If the person stole because he or she was hungry, then the person in charge of giving out the food would be punished.

Right: the keeper of the bridges. It was his duty to ensure that the rope suspension bridges were kept in good order, since they crossed deep ravines.

Writing It Down: Recording Things

Language and Writing

The Inca language, **Quechua**, was spread throughout the empire by special teachers. As everyone could speak this common language, communication and the administration of lands were made easier. However, the Incas had no system of writing.

Numbers

Quipus, consisting of a main cord plus cords of various colors, were used for counting and recording things. A group of knots placed furthest from the main cord were units, the next were tens, and the absence of a knot meant zero.

It was necessary to have a description of what was being counted in order to be able to use any quipus.

Quipu Interpreters

These were a special class of people who memorized statistical, historical, and other information and recited it when asked. They were known as quipu-kamay-us, "masters of the knotted cord" or "keeper of the quipus," experts who kept the government accounts.

Weights and Measures

Inca measurements were based on parts of the body. The span of a man's hand was equal to approximately 8 inches (20 centimeters). A fathom was equal to 64 inches (160 centimeters), which was a standard measure of land.

A pace was equal to about 4 feet (1.5 meters), and was a standard measure of distance. A topo was equal to 6,000 paces, and was used as a road distance.

A topo was also used to measure area and was thought to be the area of land enclosed by 50 fathoms × 20 fathoms. A phoqca was equal to about 26 quarts, and was a standard measure of grain.

Inca official with a quipu, which was used for counting and recording.

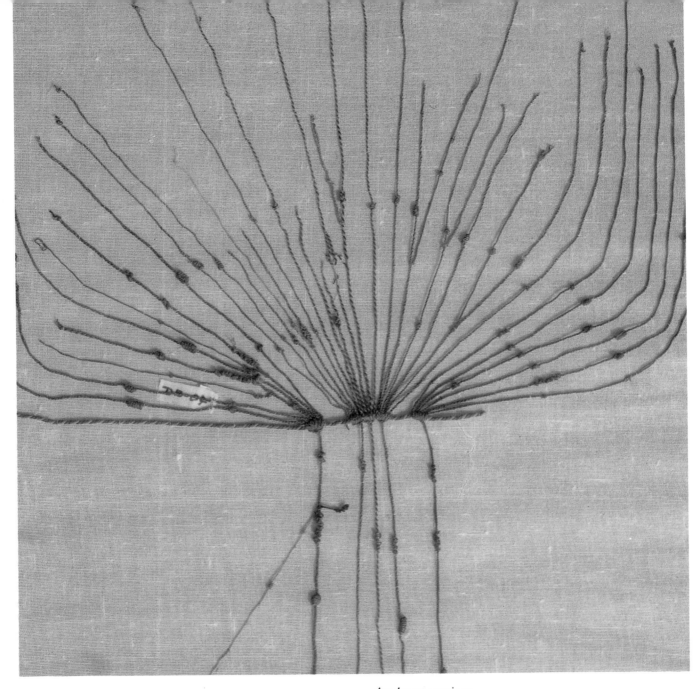

An Incan quipu.

Calendar

The Inca calendar was self-correcting. The year began at the December solstice (longest day of the year in the Southern Hemisphere). This was decided by observing the rising and setting sun through two sets of towers on either side of the capital, Cuzco, and made from a platform in the middle of the Great Square in the capital.

The year was divided into twelve months of thirty days each, and each month was made up of three ten-day weeks. The remaining five days were devoted to Inca ceremonies at the December and June solstices. The times for planting, harvesting, and ceremonies were decided by this unwritten calendar.

Inca Legends and Literature

Legends of the Incas and the people they ruled were preserved by word-of-mouth and repeated through the ages. Poets called **haravecs** chose special occasions and incidents about which to write songs and ballads and then taught them to others.

Some legends about the Inca gods, the peasant nature gods, and the prayers and hymns that were offered to them, were written down by scholars in the sixteenth and seventeenth centuries A.D. and by some Spanish missionaries. Only fragments of these legends have survived, as the Christian Spanish did everything possible to destroy the culture and pagan religion of the Incas and those they ruled. One known legend is the Legend of Viracocha, the creator god.

Viracocha turned the first people into stone statues.

The Legend

Viracocha made the heavens and the earth, as well as some human beings who were giants. He destroyed these first people as a punishment by turning them into statues. The Incas believed that the giant stone statues that can be found in Peru were these first people.

He arose again from Lake Titicaca and created at Tiahuanaco, the sun and the day and the moon and the stars. He then created from stone, men to rule over creation, women with children in cradles, and the unborn children.

Taguapica was Viracocha's son, who opposed his father. The drying up of rivers and springs created by Viracocha was said to be the work of Taguapica.

Viracocha, when his work on earth was done, waded into the sea and, using his cloak for a boat, sailed off to live in the land of the immortal until he wished to return.

Inti Illapa (the Thunder God)

This god of thunder, hail, and rain, wandered about the heavens armed with a club and a sling with which he hurled thunderbolts. His **silhouette** was outlined in the sky by the stars. He drew water from the river in the sky (the **Milky Way**) which he showered on the earth.

A Modern Inca Legend

Descendants of those who once lived in Inca lands still live in very poor and isolated conditions in settlements in the Andes. These people have myths and legends of their own which come from Inca times.

One of these legends tells how Inca-ri once founded the city of Cuzco at a place where a golden wand was stuck in the ground. Inca-ri was eventually killed by a white chief and his head buried near Lima. One day his head will be given a new body and Inca-ri will return and restore the empire of the Incas.

Art and Architecture

Architecture

The Incas built towns wherever they went. They had the supplies of raw materials needed for building and plenty of workers. Rulers had architects prepare clay models of towns or buildings. Most Inca cities were similar in appearance. All had large squares with rectangular blocks of buildings with narrow streets and a boundary wall. The local peasant inhabitants did not live in these Inca cities but in villages throughout the land.

Inca buildings were built by fitting enormous blocks of **granite** together. These were quarried nearby and transported on sledges with rollers. The blocks were raised into position by pulling them up mounds of earth. Some ruins remain, but invasions and earthquakes have destroyed most of the Incas' buildings. Most of the buildings had one story, but some were of two and three stories.

Opposite: an Inca wooden drinking vessel made in the form of a jaguar head.

Below: ruins of Machu Picchu. This city, the last of the Inca strongholds, was built high in the Andes Mountains.

Notable Inca Architecture

The Fortress of Sacsahuaman   This massive fortress overlooks Cuzco. It was built by thousands of men.

The Temple of Coricancha or "Golden Precinct"   This was the magnificent Temple at Cuzco. It consisted of a number of buildings and shrines arranged within a large wall. It contained friezes of small gold plates upon which the sun's rays shone. A garden of maize plants in the center was made of gold.

Machu Picchu   The "lost city of the Incas" occupies the summit of a steep mountain spur.

Right: Inca llama made from silver.

Below: Inca chicha jar.

Pottery

Classical Inca pottery was called imperial Cuzco. Platters and beakers and other examples have been found, mostly along routes taken by the Inca armies. Inca pottery was not made on a wheel but by carefully winding long strips of clay. Four or more colors were used to decorate the pottery, with backgrounds usually being white or red. Designs used were mainly geometric and included stylized people, animals, birds, fish, and plants.

Luxury Articles

Jewelry, finely woven materials, and ceramics were made by craftworkers in the Inca court and in the workshops of governors and local administrators. These artists were fed and clothed by the Inca. Among the items found in Inca tombs are vases of gold and silver, collars and bracelets, mirrors of polished silver, and gold masks.

Going Places: Transportation, Exploration, and Communication

Transportation of goods was done by pack animals or couriers on foot. These foot couriers could travel swiftly enough on the Inca roads to be able to transport fresh fish from the Pacific to be served on the tables at the Inca capital of Cuzco. Their main roads were built through dense jungles, as well as over high mountain ranges. Suspension bridges of twisted plants and vines (especially the thick cabuya fiber), spanning deep ravines and rivers, connected these roads.

Boats

The Incas' boats were **balsa** wood rafts or **totora** rafts made from reeds lashed together with sails attached. Some of these rafts could carry up to fifty people.

The Inca were not commercial people, so no special trade routes were developed.

The Incas used boats made from reeds lashed together. These reed boats used by Peruvian peasants today are similar to those once used by the Incas.

Roads

Armies, goods, and people could be moved quickly along the Inca roads. Two main roads ran the entire length of the empire: one along the coast and the other through the highlands. These two roads were connected to population centers by a network of smaller roads. **Tampos,** which were storehouses or shelters, were constructed at distances of one day's journey along the roads.

Some Inca roads, according to the Spanish, were wide enough to accommodate eight horsemen side-by-side and had curbs and paved sections. Trees planted along the sides shaded the travelers.

Above: a road built by the Incas. Most Inca roads were long and straight, and cobbled as shown here.

Below: Inca noble and his wife being carried on a litter.

On their tours of inspection, the Inca nobility were transported on richly decorated **sedan chairs** (or litters), which were carried on the shoulders of several bearers. An escort to protect and serve the nobility traveled alongside.

Music, Dancing, and Recreation

Hymns were sung during religious ceremonies and on other occasions, but no pure Inca music has survived. The Christian Spanish would not allow any worship of the god Viracocha, the sun god, or any of the peasant gods, and Spanish music overshadowed any Inca or peasant music. Inca music was not written down but was passed on by one person teaching another. It was very easy for the Spanish to suppress and destroy it.

The Spanish church authorities demanded the suppression of dances, songs, and ancient taquis (dances), and ordered the burning of all musical instruments.

However, Inca music did not disappear entirely. The Inca music was integrated into the Spanish music, but because it was so different and played on different instruments having a certain tone and range, experts can distinguish this music from the European influenced music.

Inca instruments included the pan pipes, trumpets, drums, and flutes.

Opposite: music and dancing were a part of Inca ceremonies. The Inti Raimi Pageant—Festival of the Sun God—is still celebrated in Peru today.

Below: Inca fiesta showing woman with drum and men with pipes.

Wars and Battles

The Inca Conquests

The expansion of the Inca land began when a people called the Chancas appeared at the western edge of the Inca lands in the fifteenth century A.D., and in 1438, attacked the Incas. There were two Inca strongholds, at Cuzco and at Calca, but these were reunited under a single leader after the Chancas entered into an agreement with the Incas. In spite of this agreement, the Chancas remained a threat and more battles followed.

The Incas also led successful campaigns against the Colla and the Lupaca, which gave the Incas control of more land. The Inca territory was expanded even further by Topa Inca Yupanqui, son of Pachacuti Inca Yupanqui, who led armies against the Chimú as far north as Quito (Ecuador). Attacks against the Chimú were made from sea and land at the same time. The Incas captured the Chimú capital of Chan Chan and returned south to bring the whole area under Inca control.

In 1476, Topa Inca Yupanqui (then leader of the Incas) led expeditions against the people in the valleys of southern Peru, which then became part of the Inca empire. The people of the Cañete Valley resisted the Incas for three years.

Huayna Capac succeeded Topa Inca Yupanqui and his reign was peaceful, except for the conquest of Chachapoyas in northeastern Peru and later northern Ecuador. The Chiriguano invaded Inca frontier settlements from time to time but were driven out, and forts were built along the frontier.

While Huayna Capac was on an expedition in the north, he received word that an epidemic had broken out at Quito (on the way to Cuzco) and went to investigate. He died during this epidemic. This was probably smallpox or

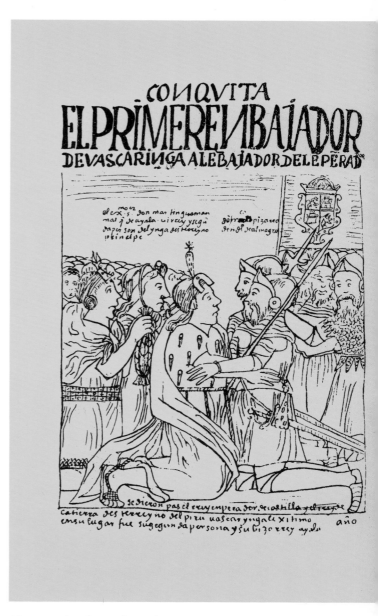

Above: the Spanish ambassador and his soldiers meet the Inca nobles for the first time.

measles, which were European diseases brought into South America by the Spanish and probably passed on via the Chiriguano who had been in contact with them. There was no recognized successor to Huaya Capac and civil war soon broke out, with the armies of Huascar and Atahuallpa causing much death and destruction.

The Spanish

The Spanish, who had landed on the northern coast of Peru in 1532, attempted to arrange a meeting with Atahuallpa in order to kidnap him. Atahuallpa was seeking the Spanish as allies in his civil war, but he was tricked by them because they only wanted the Inca gold. Atahuallpa was kidnapped and killed by the Spanish. Various men wanted to be the next Inca leader, but finally, Manco Inca Yupanqui became ruler, with Spanish permission.

Manco was mistreated by the Spanish. He escaped and led attacks against the Spanish but was finally defeated. He fled and set up an Inca city in the mountains.

The Spanish conquered the Inca lands over the next few years.

Meeting between the Inca king and a Spanish conquistador.

Arms and Armor

Inca soldiers were organized according to their arms. Bronze- or bone-tipped spears, arrows (although bows and arrows were not used by the mountain tribes), slings, and the bola were the main arms. Wooden swords with serrated edges and clubs with stone and spiked metal heads were used for hand-to-hand fighting.

Weapons of the Inca nobility were mounted with gold and silver and their helmets were adorned with precious stones and feathers from tropical birds.

Armor consisted of helmets made of wood or animal skins, cloth tunics padded with cotton, and round or square shields. The Spanish later adopted this armor.

Returning Armies

The heads of opponents who had been defeated were placed on spears and held in the air by soldiers entering Cuzco. Cups for drinking were made from victims' skulls. Some opponents were whipped and their skins made into drums. Necklaces were made from enemies' teeth.

Inca Inventions and Special Skills

Spread of Tools and Techniques

Differences exist in the types of materials and techniques that were used to make tools. Before a land was conquered, metal was mainly used for ornaments and wood and stone for tools. After the Incas came, copper and bronze were substituted. Tools such as crowbars, chisels, axes, knives, and club heads were fashioned out of copper and bronze. Wood-burning furnaces usually were located on hillsides to supply a constant draft that would keep the fire hot enough to melt metal.

Road Building

The system of roads allowed people to move quickly from one part of the empire to another. Armies could be moved quickly and so could goods and people. Relay runners carried messages from the provinces to Cuzco. Shelters and storehouses, or tampos, built at distances of one day's travel made this movement even easier.

Stone Architecture

Buildings in the Inca cities were made from huge blocks of stone (usually granite). Some of them were 15 feet (5 meters) high. They were placed accurately on top of and alongside each other. Thousands of peasant workmen hauled these huge blocks along a series of rollers. To reach greater heights the blocks were hauled up ramps of earth. The Inca methods of building were similar to those of the Egyptians.

Quipus

As described earlier, quipus were used for counting and calculation, although piles of stones and a device like an abacus served the same purposes. Quipus consisted of a main cord strung with other cords in various colors with knots tied at intervals. The distance between the knots and the way they were arranged indicated certain numbers. Quipus are still used today for counting the size of herds in some places in the Andes.

Cultivated Potato

The peasants of Peru under Inca control cultivated many lands and crops. Originally the potato was only as big as a nut and grew in the wild. Over time it was cultivated and developed into about 700 different varieties suited to different climates and purposes.

Irrigation Systems

The peasants were taught how to irrigate their farmlands so food could be produced during dry times. They learned how to build tunnels, aqueducts of stone, dams, and canals to bring water from rivers to the farms. They also learned to use the melting snow of the Andes for irrigation.

A United People

The Inca leaders managed to unite people of quite different cultures, religions, and languages into one empire. They did this by giving these conquered people one religion and one language, and by treating them well. Even though conquered people were allowed to keep their own traditions, they had to worship the Inca, the sun god, and other Inca

Inca buildings were made from huge blocks of stone, as shown in this Inca wall. Some of the stones had twelve corners as shown in the inset.

gods. Special teachers were sent to all the conquered lands to teach everyone a common language, Quechua.

The Incas looked after the people they conquered, too. All the land belonged to the government. The people were told when to plant and how much to plant. At harvest time they were told how much they could keep. The government made sure that everyone had enough food.

Why the Civilization Declined

The Inca civilization was destroyed by the Spanish who came in search of gold. They conquered the Incas and then tried to replace the Inca and peasant religions with Christianity.

The natives accepted the Spanish Christianity in much the same way as they had accepted the religion of the Incas. It was practiced along with pagan religions and did not really change the natives' beliefs. However, when the Spanish discovered this, they punished those who still practiced their old religion.

Contagious diseases, such as smallpox, measles, and malaria, were brought into the population by the Spanish and killed many of the Inca people.

The Spanish also took over the Inca custom of mit'a (a form of taxation), and later forced the people to work in the mines where many of them died. Men in the mines had to produce twenty-five sacks of ore, each weighing 100 pounds (45 kilograms), in twelve hours. They worked in narrow tunnels with only candles for light. Many natives fled so they would not have to work in the mines, and others sold their wives and children in their place. The Spanish also forced the native peo-

Peruvian peasants today, threshing grain. The peaks of the Andes Mountains rise high in the background.

ple to work in the weaving and pottery workshops and made them carry heavy loads.

It is thought that half of the native population died as a result of the Spanish invading their lands.

Even though Manco Inca Yupanqui managed to flee from the Spanish and to establish an Inca city in the mountains, from where he led expeditions against the Spanish, this was in vain. The Spanish eventually dominated the South American lands. Children of the Incas were given a Spanish Catholic education, and soon the old Inca ways were changed and the civilization began to disappear.

However, the descendants of those who resided in Inca lands today live in settlements in the Andes. These people are poor and isolated. They are suspicious of strangers and still pray and make sacrifices to their traditional gods and huacas. They still speak the Inca language, Quechua. The Inca civilization has not completely died out.

The Inca civilization and culture were destroyed by the Spanish who replaced Inca religions with Christianity. This Spanish church in Cuzco, Peru, was built upon the Inca Temple of the Sun.

Glossary

Adobe Sun-dried bricks of mud, silt, or clay deposited by rivers.

Alpaca A South American animal that produces wool. Its coat is usually dark brown or black but can be lighter. The wool is very light. Some alpacas grow very long coats that touch the ground as they walk.

Amulet A charm or object kept or worn by people in the belief that it will keep evil spirits away.

Aqueduct An artificial channel made to take water over a valley or ravine.

Balsa A tree which grows in South America. The wood of this tree is very light and is used to make rafts.

Bola A weapon used by the Indians in South America. It consisted of two or more heavy balls tied to the ends of long strong cords. It would be thrown at an animal or person, who would become entangled and fall.

Chicha Maize beer.

Conopas Religious amulets owned by a family.

Curacas Elders of a farming community who became administrators to the Incas.

Divination Superstitious appeal to the spirits to uncover things hidden. These appeals included listening to oracles or spirits in temples, studying the movements of spiders and the entrails of animals, or counting the grains on a cob of maize.

Friar A member of certain Christian religious orders.

Glacier A slow-moving river of ice.

Granite A granular, hard rock used for buildings and monuments. The rock is very hard and is not easily worn away by wind and water.

Guano A rich fertilizer obtained from the droppings of sea birds.

Haravec A name given during Inca times to poets who composed songs, poems, and ballads about great and important events.

Huacas Sacred or holy things. It also means "the spirits that live in things or places" such as waterfalls, mountains, and shrines.

Kumbi Material woven from fine vicuña wool.

Llama A South American animal used as a pack animal. It was also a source of food, wool, hides, tallow (for candles), and fuel (from dried dung). These animals stand about 48 inches (120 centimeters) tall. They can be white, black, brown, or white with black or brown markings. Their fleece is coarser than that of alpacas.

Llautu Narrow band of many colors worn around the head as a symbol of rank.

Milky Way This is the name given to the great arc of stars and dust, which can be seen clearly in the night sky.

Okra Tall plant of the mallow family that can be eaten.

Paqarina Holes in the ground through which, many ancient people believed, their ancestors emerged. These places were regarded as shrines. The Inca paqarina was at Paqari-tampu, a short distance from Cuzco.

Peccary Four-footed South American animal, similar to a pig.

Poncho A blanketlike cloak with a hole in the center for the head to go through.

Quechua The Inca language.

Quipu A device consisting of a cord with knotted strings of various colors attached used for recording events and keeping accounts.

Raymi The name given to an Inca religious festival to worship the sun god.

Sedan chair A portable chair without wheels for one or more persons. The chair was suspended on poles and carried by two or more men, in front and behind. It was used by the Inca nobles and administrators for transportation.

Silhouette An outline or a dark image outlined against a lighter background.

Sitowa The name given to the great Inca festival held to chase away evil spirits.

Sling A weapon used for hurling stones that was made of a strap with two strings attached for holding the stone. The ends were attached to a stick or held in place by one hand. The sling was whirled rapidly to release the stone. When used properly, this weapon could kill a horse or break an iron sword.

Talisman A stone, ring, or other object with figures or characters carved into it or a carved shape. It was believed to have the power to keep evil spirits away.

Tampo The storehouse or shelter which was placed along Inca roads at intervals of one day's journey.

Totora A boat made of reeds tied together.

Turf sods Blocks of earth with a covering of grass that has the matted roots of the grass in it.

Vicuña An animal native to the Andean region of South America. It stands about 31 inches (80 centimeters) high. The vicuña's wool varies from a light cinnamon color to off-white and is silkier and finer than sheep's wool.

The Incas: Some Famous People and Places

ATAHUALLPA

Atahuallpa was the last ruler of the Inca empire before it was taken over by the Spanish conquistador Francisco Pizarro. He was the son of Huayna Capac and after having fought and deposed his brother, Huascar, Atahuallpa became leader in 1532, just before the Spanish invasion. Atahuallpa refused to become a Christian or acknowledge the King of Spain as his king. He was taken prisoner by Pizarro and executed by strangulation on August 29, 1533.

FRANCISCO PIZARRO

Francisco Pizarro was the Spanish conqueror of the Incas. He was joined in his exploits by four of his brothers and set sail with one ship, 180 men, and 37 horses. Later, two more ships joined the expedition. They made contact with Atahuallpa, the leader of the Incas, and his army of some 30,000.

A meeting between Atahuallpa and Pizarro was arranged. The Inca leader was carried on a litter and escorted by 3,000 to 4,000 armed men into the city of Cajamarca. Vincente de Valverde was sent to demand that Atahuallpa accept Christianity and acknowledge King Charles V of Spain as his master, both of which Atahuallpa refused. Pizarro then ordered an attack on the Inca party. Pizarro, himself, seized Atahuallpa who was held hostage and later put to death. When the Inca armies heard of their leader's death, they retreated, allowing Pizarro to proceed to Cuzco.

CUZCO

This was the capital city and holy city of the Inca empire and dates from the eleventh century A.D. The city today contains many Inca ruins, including the Fortress of Sacsahuaman and the famous Temple of the Sun. Pizarro's Spanish forces occupied and plundered Cuzco in 1533. Cuzco is still the principal Andean center of Peru.

CAJAMARCA

This was the ancient Inca city where the Inca chief, Atahuallpa, was captured by Pizarro in 1533. Here, while being held hostage, the Inca leader promised Pizarro as much gold as he could fit in his cell in exchange for his freedom. Pizarro agreed to the offer, but after receiving the gold, killed Atahuallpa anyway.

Today, Cajamarca is the principal center of the northern Andes.

MANCO CAPAC

Manco Capac was the founder of the Inca dynasty and was also known as Manqo Qhapaq. Legend says that he, his three brothers, and four sisters emerged from a cave at Paqari-tampu (Paccari Tampu), and after wandering with the Inca people, Capac eventually became their leader. He named his eldest son, Sinchi Roca, to succeed him.

MACHU PICCHU

This is the ancient fortress city of the Incas and is often referred to as the "lost city of the Incas." It lies in the Andes Mountains to the northwest of Cuzco. The Spanish failed to find this city which remained hidden until 1911, when it was discovered by Hiram Bingham of Yale University. The city contains a temple and a citadel. The city consists of five square miles (thirteen square kilometers) of terraces with 3,000 steps connecting these terraces. Many small houses made from unmortared stone were built here.

LAKE TITICACA

This is the world's highest lake that can be navigated by large vessels. It lies 12,500 feet (3,810 meters) above sea level in the Andes Mountains.

Near this lake, according to Inca legend, the children of the sun drove their golden wedge into the ground and settled. Along the shores of this lake are ruins, some of which are thought to predate the Incas.

VIRACOCHA INCA

Viracocha Inca, leader of the Incas in the early part of the fifteenth century, brought about changes in Inca administration and, as a result, made the Incas more powerful. Before the time of Viracocha Inca, when neighboring groups were conquered, the lands were taken but the people were otherwise left undisturbed. Under Viracocha Inca, permanent rule was established over conquered lands. Viracocha Inca was assisted in his plan by his uncles, Vicaquirao and Apo Mayta.

TOPA INCA YUPANQUI

Topa Inca Yupanqui (Thupa 'Inka Yupanki), son of Pachacuti Inca Yupanqui, led expeditions through Inca lands and outflanked the enemy Chimú armies. The Incas were able to conquer the Chimú and sack their capital at Chan Chan. They then advanced south to Pachacamac and brought further lands under Inca control. In about 1471, Topa Inca Yupanqui succeeded his father and became ruler of the Incas. Among his administrative achievements was a system for classifying the adult male population into units ranging from 100 to 10,000 people, and from these groupings, labor and conscripts for the army were recruited and assigned. He also introduced a system whereby each province had to produce women to serve in the temples or to become wives of soldiers who had proven themselves in war. Topa Inca Yupanqui died unexpectedly in 1493, before the successor to his leadership had been decided.

TEMPLE OF THE SUN

This is the famous Inca temple at Cuzco, where pilgrims came from the furthest corners of the Inca empire. This temple was the most magnificent structure in the New World.

The base of the Temple of the Sun was plated in gold in some places and was used as a foundation for the Church of Santo Domingo.

Index